Hello and welcome back, before I start t
new recipes, I would like to say a huge thank you to everyone
who bought my first book and gave me the confidence to write
book no 2.

Unfortunately, I am having to self-publish again via Amazon,
so I have no control over the print quality or the cost. Amazon
print each book individually and they charge £5.20 for every
book they print, then there is the page count I can't go over
100 pages, or it zooms the selling price to £20 per book which
is just not acceptable.

Then after they have printed the book and charged me for
this, they also then charge me to sell it to you so I earn £2.60
per book sold. I appreciate the cost of my books can seem
high in comparison to others within the genre, but we aren't
comparing "apples with apples" I don't have a publishing
company behind me printing off 1000s of copies and helping
with the marketing to sell the book.

It's just me, my phone and my fat finger lol, all recipes are
mine, cooked by me, all photographs were style by me taken
by me and all food eaten by Graeme and I.

However, without the Amazon Self-Publishing Programme I
would not have been able to publish any cookbooks so for
that I am thankful of their services.

This table shows you the breakdown of costs from
Amazon and the royalties I earn per book.

kindle direct publishing | royalty calculator

Figures generated by this tool are for estimation purposes only. Your actual royalty will be calculated when you set up your book.

1. Enter interior type:	Color Ink
2. Enter number of pages:	100
3. Choose a distribution channel:	Amazon.co.uk
4. Enter anticipated list price (£):	£12.99

Printing cost:	£5.20	
Minimum list price:	£8.67	
Amazon royalty:	£2.60	
Expanded Distribution royalty:	-£0.01	*List Price is too low for Expanded Distribution

Lighter Bites is all about taking your cooking into the Summer months and making delicious, tasty food without spending hours in a hot kitchen. We have some Summer Slow Cooker recipes, some 15–30 minute recipes, some Summer Puddings, and of course Fakeaways so something for everyone.

For those who follow me on Instagram and Facebook I am still following the Slimming World diet so once again some of the ingredients can seem a little strange, when you see this you can either follow the recipe or substitute the ingredient to suit your diet plan.

Calories are included for each recipe BUT NOT THE OIL as we all use different oil and different pans which can make a huge difference to how much you need, so you will need to add this value into every recipe. I have also included what I'm calling a "swap in / swap out" section an example of this would be where the recipe states cornflakes you may want to use breadcrumbs so I'm going to give you the value for the cornflakes separately and you can decide to either leave them in or swap them out.

I cannot include SYN values as this is a copyright protected word and system owned by Slimming World.

Throughout the book I have tried to use "common ingredients" between recipes for example when using yogurt, I have used the same brand / type in all the recipes as this cuts down on food waste.

With Lighter Bites I have tried to create Mix & Match recipes so there is a section for sides that will go with any of the recipes within the book.

Unfortunately, the "chatty" side from my first book is somewhat missing from this book as I just don't have the space to waffle on, but I'm hoping the recipes make up for the lack of chit chat.

OK let's get cooking! As we need to shoehorn as many recipes as possible into the space available – it is going to be a challenge lol xxx

Contents

PASTA DISHES

I think during the Summer pasta features heavily in our diet mainly because its easy to cook and super filling.

I am going to use these header pages to give you any hints and tips for the recipes within this section as space is premium and I can't always fit in extra information under each recipe.

GNOCCHI- a question I always get asked is what is it??? Its potato dumplings and comes in both fresh and cooked, the fresh is in the chiller isle and the cooked is with the pasta in supermarkets.

If you are going to use cooked gnocchi boil and drain it first, how do you know when its cooked??? It floats to the top of the water it literally takes minutes to cook.

Whatever you do not overcook it as it becomes really starchy and gloopy however, when cooked properly it's a fantastic ingredient to use.

You can always swap gnocchi for pasta in any recipe if you are unsure.

In Lighter Bites I have used Lemons in lots of recipes and over the years I have found that some British Lemons are amazing and others not so much, so before you use them have a little taste and decide how they settle on your tastebuds if they are super strong then use sparingly as you do not want to overpower the recipe.

All the pasta recipes can be made and stored in an airtight container in the fridge for up to 3 days making them perfect for quick lunch.

The other common ingredient used throughout the pasta section is Philadelphia lightest as it is the most used amongst dieters but as always use any cream cheese you like.

SUMMER PASTA

There are no rules as to what you add but we both really enjoyed it, it wasn't over filling or too heavy a perfect lunch idea. I also created a dressing which works beautifully with the pasta, but I am leaving this to you to decide whether you want to use it or not.

There is also a note on the recipe regarding Edamame Beans which I love but they are so expensive I now use Frozen Baby Broad Beans – trust me you will not notice the difference.

SUMMER PASTA

INGREDIENTS SERVES 2

160g Dry Pasta
80g Edamame Beans OR Frozen Baby Broad Beans
200g Small Tin of Sweetcorn
1 Red Pepper
! Small Carrot
Half a Red Onion
2" Piece of Cucumber
6 Cherry Tomatoes
Basil OPTIONAL

DRESSING
20 Sprays of Extra Virgin Olive Oil
1.5 Teaspoons of lemon Juice
1 Teaspoon of White Wine Vinegar
Pinch of Peper

Cook the pasta as per the manufacturers instructions
Once cooked drain run under cold water
Chop all vegetables
If using frozen baby broad beans defrost them
Julienne the carrot (long thin strips)
Mix the pasta with the vegetables
Mix the dressing if you are using it and add
it to the salad
If using Basil add it toward the end and mix
it through

Calories 465 per portion   Dressing 21 Calories per portion

LEMON CHICKEN PASTA

This recipe screams Summer on a plate and it was so easy to make the perfect recipe for a balmy Summers Eve.

My top tip for this recipe is the lemons you use some lemons don't really have lots of taste and most of the flavour usually comes from the zest which is where the essential oils are. So, keep tasting the sauce to ensure you get the taste you want you can always add more lemon juice at the end of cooking if you are usure.

LEMON CHICKEN PASTA
INGREDIENTS SERVES 2

2 Chicken Breast Or 400g Chicken Strips
160g Dry Tagliatelle Pasta
2 Tablespoons of Philadelphia Lightest
1 Lemon
Half a Vegetable Stock Pot
150ml Water
Basil to Garnish OPTIONAL

If using Chicken breast cut into slices this will help reduce
the cooking time
Spray a pan with oil on a medium heat add the chicken
and season with salt & pepper cook for 5 minutes
Dissolve half a vegetable stock pot into 150ml of boiling water
Add stock to frying pan and bring to a low rolling bubble to
finish cooking the chicken.
Add 2 Tablespoons of Philadelphia stir well this creates
the creamy sauce
Add the rind of 1 lemon and the juice of 1 lemon mix well
Boil and drain the pasta keep a cup of pasta water
If the sauce becomes to thick add a splash of pasta water
You can either serve the creamy chicken in top of the
tagliatelle or add the tagliatelle to the pan and mix it all through

Calories 545 per portion

MAC CHEESE WITH BACON CRUMB

I appreciate that this recipe sounds bonkers but trust me it tastes amazing. As some of you may know Graeme "apparently" doesn't like cheese, however he ate this no problem and now likes Mac Cheese, well this version of it, which tells me he really does like cheese!

This recipe is by no means authentic, but it ticks all the boxes for taste and ease of cooking.

MAC CHEESE WITH BACON CRUMB

INGREDIENTS SERVES 2

160g Dry Macaroni Pasta
4 Bacon Mediallions
75g Philadelphia Lightest
40g Grated Cheese I used Double Gloucester
Keep 1 Cup of pasta water

Cook the pasta as per the manufacturers instructions
Once cooked drain but keep a cup of the water
Grill the bacon so its just starting to crisp
Once cooked add it to a blender and blend
into a crumb texture
Add Philadelphia to the pasta and mix well
together with approx 150mil of water
start with 100ml then add more if needed
remember this needs to be grilled so the mixture
needs to be slightly looser as the heat will
asborb some of the liquid.
Pour into an ovenproof dish and top with the
grated cheese and the bacon crumb
Place under the grill until the bacon is golden
and crisp.

Calories 485 per portion

MOZZARELLA & CHORIZO GNOCCHI BAKE

A classic but with a twist using fresh gnocchi which makes this the perfect "one pan dish" I used fresh gnocchi which is found in the chilled isle this cooks from the packet within the sauce. If you are using cooked gnocchi from the pasta isle, then I would suggest you boil it first then add it to the sauce.

In this recipe I used a Mozzarella ball but you can just use grated mozzarella if you wish.

MOZZARELLA & CHORIZO GNOCCHI BAKE

INGREDIENTS SERVES 2

400g Fresh Gnocchi (Chilled Isle)
1 Small Onion
1 Tin of Chopped Tomatoes
50g Chorizo
70g Mozzarella
1 Tablespoon of Balsamic Vinegar
2 Teaspoons of Lazy Garlic
2 Teaspoons of Italian Herbs
Small bunch of Basil

Finely dice the onion
In a frying pan sprayed with oil soften the onion
Chop the chorizo and add it to the pan and cook
for 5minutes to release the oils
Add the tinned tomatoes
Add the garlic
Add the balsamic vinegar
Roughly Chop the Basil (golf ball size) and add it
to the pan
Add the gnocchi and mix everything ensure the
gnocchi is coated
Chop 50g of the Mozzarella into small cubes and add
it to the pan
Cook on a medium heat until the gnocchi is cooked,
If the sauce becomes too thick add a splash of
water
Taste the sauce and adjust if needed this will
depend on the brand of tinned tomatoes you are
using you may need to add more balsamic vinegar
Add the remaining Mozzarella to the top and pop
it under the grill to melt the cheese

Calories 525 per portion

CREAMY SPICY SAUSAGE PASTA

This is the perfect one pot recipe so easy to make, although I have added chilli sauce to this pasta dish you can make this recipe to suit your taste so either reduce the chilli or add more.

I used Sriracha Chilli Sauce which I find really powerful in spice and heat, but you can use any chilli sauce you like or even just a sprinkle of mild chilli powder.

SPICY SAUSAGE PASTA
INGREDIENTS SERVES 2

160g Dry Pasta
4 Chicken Sausages (I used Heck Chicken Italia)
3 Tablespoons of Philadelphia Lightest
50g Edamame Beans
1 Onion
1 Pepper
1 Tablespoon Tomato Puree
Half a Tablespoon of Sriracha Sauce (Chilli Sauce)
1 Teaspoon of Lazy Garlic
200ml Water
Salt & Pepper

Finely slice the onion
Chop the pepper
Cook the pasta according to the manufacturers instructions
In a large frying pan sprayed with oil add the onions
and peppers
Add the sausages to the pan also
Cook everything on a low heat until the onions are soft
and the sausages are cooked
Drain the pasta and keep 200ml of the water
Add the pasta to the frying pan
Add the Philadelphia
Add the edamame beans
Add the garlic
Add the water start with 150ml stir everything through
the water creates the creamy sauce add more if needed.
Add the Sriracha NOTE if you are not keen on hot spicy foods
you can either start with a small amount of chilli sauce and keep
tasting until you get to the taste you like.
OR add a mild chilli powder this will be lower in heat than the
srircha sauce.

Calories 519 per portion

10 MINUTE LASAGNE

This recipe was born on a hot summer day a couple of years ago and Graeme wanting lasagne.

The base of this recipe is my slow cooker spag bol, you will find the recipe for this under the slow cooker section this makes 4 portions which I freeze in portions of 2.

This is a huge cheat I defrost the spag bol use 1 lasagne sheet and use cream cheese to create the white sauce, yes I know sounds terrible but trust me try it.

10 MINUTE LASAGNE

INGREDIENTS SERVES 1

1 Portion of Slow Cooker Spaghetti Bolognese
1 Lasagne Sheet
2 Tablespoons of Philadelphia Lightest
50g Mozzerella

If needed snap the lasagne sheet to fit the ovenproof
dish you are using
Soak the lasagne sheet in boiling water to soften it slightly
In an individual ovenproof dish add a slightly warmed
portion of spag bol
Add the lasange sheet
Mix the philadelphia with a dash of warm water to create
a creamy sauce texture
Cover the lasagne sheet with the sauce
Add the mozzerella
Either put into the oven or under the grill on 180 degrees for
approx 10mins to melt the cheese.

Calories 440 per portion

FISH SECTION

If you look at my Social Media Pages you will see fish is missing! I'm not a huge fish fan, I do try but It would never be my first choice in a restaurant or at home.

However, my inbox is always full of requests for fish recipes and whilst I'm not keen, Graeme loves fish of any kind. So, in the book I decided to dive in and create a few recipes that I hope will tickle your tastebuds.

I must admit I enjoyed them all which was a bit of a shock to be honest. The only recipe that really wasn't for me was the salmon – it was "too fishy" lol I tried it but Graeme was the main taste tester for this recipe and give it a huge thumbs up.

The fish pie recipe was really good, and this will be a recipe I will make again but next time I will use a seafood mix its less faff and probably cheaper.

FISH KEBABS – as the recipe states if you use cod it can fall apart during the grilling and fall off the skewers mine held together well but its just worth noting when buying the fish for this recipe. The Tikka spice I used was just a supermarket own brand these spices vary hugely in their potency so taste them first before adding them to the fish.

CRISPY FISH BURGER – now this one I will eat no problem it was really good. My top tip is before you start cooking the fish sit it on some kitchen roll to try and removed as much liquid as possible. This will really help when you come to dipping the fish into the egg then into the cornflakes.

TANDOOR FISH KEBABS

I have always wanted to try fish kebabs and to be honest they were really good and the Tandoor spice worked so well with the fish. There is a note in my recipe about using Cod to make kebabs it may flake as you cook it hence me stating using Monkfish but as always use what you like and what is within your budget.

TANDOORI FISH KEBABS
INGREDIENTS SERVES 2

400g Monkfish, you can use cod but it may flake during cooking
3 Tablespoons of 0% Fat Free Greek Yogurt
1 Tablespoon of Tandoori Spice
Juice of half a lemon
Rind of half lemon
Half a teaspoon of Lazy Garlic

Ensure there are no bones in the fish
Pat the fish dry removing as much moisture
as possible
Mix the marinate in a bowl and taste making sure
it suits your taste before adding it to the fish
Cut the fish into chunky cubes - don't cut it too
small as you will dry it out during cooking
Add the fish to the marinate then place in the
fridge for a minimum of 30 minutes
Thread the fish onto wooden skewers
Cook under a grill on 180 degrees for approx 15mins
turing during the cooking. The cooking time will
depend on how big you cut the fish cubes into

Calories 164 per portion

HONEY SOY SALMON

This was beautiful such fantastic flavours and a perfect Summer recipe. The key with this recipe is to leave the Salmon to marinate as long as possible. My other tip is once the Salmon is cooked and you are reducing the leftover marinate, do not take your eyes off the pan the sauce will reduce quickly and becomes very sticky which is perfect for drizzling over the fish.

HONEY SOY SALMON
INGREDIENTS SERVES 2

260g (2 Fillets) Salmon
2 Tablespoons of Honey
2 Tablespoon of Soy
1 Teaspoon of Garlic
1 Teaspoon of fresh Ginger

Grate the ginger
Add to a bowl the soy, honey, ginger and garlic
taste and adjust if needed.
Add the Salmon to a dish and pour over the marinate
pop in the fridge for a minimum of 30minutes
In a large frying pan sprayed with oil on a medium
heat add the salmon fillets skin side down and
cook slowly
Keep the leftover marinate you will need this later
Once the salmon has started to cook from the bottom
place it under the grill on 180 degrees keep cooking
until you see the cooking lines on the side of the
salmon starting to meet in the middle once you see this
stop cooking.
Don't overcook the salmon
Remove the salmon from the pan and set aside
Add the remaining marinate to the pan on a
medium heat reduce the sauce until it becomes
thick and sticky pour it over the salmon.

Calories 287 per portion

FISH PIE

This was one of my favourite fish recipes I had 3 portions! I have never made fish pie before, but I will be making it again.

With this recipe you can add a squeeze of lemon juice I added lemon zest the reason for this is lemon juice can split the sauce it wont change the taste and will still be perfectly fine to eat. As always, I will leave this decision to you, again we are back to taste, taste and taste again to suit your tastebuds.

FISH PIE
INGREDIENTS SERVES 4

600g Potatoes
250g White Fish I used Cod
180g Uncooked Pawns OR you can use a frozen fish pie mix
1 Leek
3 Tablespoons of Philadelphia Lightest
100g Cheese I used Double Gloucester
Half a Vegetable Stock Pot
Rind of Half a lemon
200g Peas
150ml Water
Salt & Pepper

Peel and dice potatoes cook in pan of boiling water
Once cooked drain leave to steam this will ensure you
remove as much water as possible.
If using frozen fish defrost and remove as much liquid as possible
Chop fish into chunks
Chop leek
Spray a pan with spray oil and soften leek. Set some aside as this will be
added to the potatoes
Add the fish and prawns to the pan cook on a low heat
Add vegetable stock pot and 150ml water
Add Philadelphia and mix well
Add Zest of lemon
Add peas
Don't over cook the fish as soon as the prawns
turn pink stop cooking
Season and taste adjust if needed
Ladle out the fish add it to a pie dish and ladle over the creamy sauce
mixture, press it down
To your potatoes add the leeks you set aside,
grate the cheese add this to the potatoes and mash
Add mash to top of fish then pop under grill 200 degrees
unti potato top is crispy and slightly browned

Calories 413 per portion

CRISPY FISH BURGER

Now these were really special and if I can get one non fish lover like myself to try just one fish recipe from my book then please try this one! It was amazing and I can guarantee I will be making these lots over the Summer months.

You can change the flavours if you like for me there was just enough of a "hint" of spices but not enough to overpower the fish.

CRISPY FISH BURGER
INGREDIENTS SERVES 2

400g (2 Fillets) Cod or any White Fish
50g Cornflakes
1 Egg
Half a Teaspoon of Paprika
Zest of half a Lemon
A good pinch of Salt & Pepper

Whisk the egg
Crush the cornflakes but dont crush them to dust
leave some larger pieces
Add the paprika and lemon zest to the cornflakes
and mix well
Pat dry the fish with kitchen roll
try to remove as much moisture as
possible
Dip the fish into the egg then into the cornflakes
Place onto a baking tray sprayed with oil
Spray the top of the fish
Cook in the oven on 170 degrees for approx 15mins
or until the fish is cooked this will depend on the
thickness of the fillet you are using. Turn the fish
half way through cooking to crisp the bottom.

Calories 202 per portion Swap in/out 83 cals for cornflakes

FAKEAWAYS

As you know I am a huge Fakeaway fan and in the summer months I get to eat my all time favourite food Kebabs, I really could eat these everyday of the week.

I have tried to add as much variety into this section as possible as during the Summer eating outside will feature high on our wish lists.

All kebabs, burgers, koftas and pizza's can be cooked on a BBQ for the purpose of Lighter Bites I cooked them all in the oven or under a grill – plus it was February and March so definitely not BBQ weather lol.

ZINGER BURGER – I have used cornflakes in this recipe they also feature in other recipes throughout the book because they really do give the best crunch.

You can swap these for breadcrumbs if you wish or use whatever you wish to suit your diet plan.

Wherever cornflakes appear in a recipe the calories are listed separately to allow you to either add them into the recipe or swap them for say breadcrumbs.

PORK & APPLE BURGER – pork mice can be very coarse, so I have suggested you pulse it in a blender to break down the meat slightly. This will really help the burgers hold together better.

LIME AND CORIANDER BURGER – a fantastic recipe and beautiful flavours definitely worth trying. My top tip is to not over blend the chicken as it will go to mush and you will find it difficult to shape the burgers and to get them to hold firm during cooking. All burgers need chilling in the fridge before cooking this really does help them stay together and especially if you are cooking them on the BBQ.

27

KOFTAS - after years of making these and them falling off the skewers I have finally cracked them lol. I found that taking a golf ball size of the mixture and squishing it in your fingers a couple of times brings the mix together better. Then rolling it into a ball then into a sausage shape really seemed to do the trick, normally I would form the koftas around the skewer and I think this was always my mistake.

For this batch I inserted the skewer through the middle of the kofta once they were formed. Now im sure 99% of you already do this – so this tip is for the 1% of people like me who didn't know.

KEBABS & GYROS – always try to marinate the chicken for as long as possible overnight in the fridge would be best if you have the time. My top tip is not to cut the chicken into small cubes as it will dry out during cooking and no one likes tough chewy chicken.

The chicken is marinated in yogurt and spices the yogurt is there to protect the chicken from drying out and during the cooking the yogurt sets and hardens, and the chicken stays moist.

ZINGER BURGER – again I have used cornflakes for the added crunch, but you can swap them for breadcrumbs. When mixing the spices together taste the mix and ensure it suits your taste don't worry if you think it's a little powerful the spices get mixed into the cornflakes so the taste gets somewhat diluted.

BURGERS – you will see I never use an egg to bind my burgers together. I usually find that if you blend an onion until it starts to release its juices that is enough to hold them together, but as always if you want to use an egg then the choice is yours.

CHICKEN TIKKA KEBABS

My favourite every food, Kebabs I could eat these everyday of the week no problem at all. I make these often on my Facebook page but decided they needed to be in Lighter Bites because kebabs are perfect Summer food and they are so easy to make.

CHICKEN TIKKA KEBABS

INGREDIENTS SERVES 2

500g Chicken you can use thigh or breast
3 Tablespoons of 0% Fat Free Greek Yogurt
2 Tablespoons of Mild Tikka Powder
1 Teaspoon of Lazy Garlic
Zest of Half a Lemon
Juice of Half a Lemon

Chop chicken into large chunks
Add the yogurt, Tikka powder, garlic and lemon Zest and
juice to a bowl and mix well
Taste the marinate is it to your liking? if not adjust
Add the chicken to the marinate and ensure its fully covered
Cover and place into the fridge for a minimum of 30minutes
longer if possible overnight would be best.
Thread the chicken onto skewers
Pop under the grill until cooked set the grill at 180 degrees
keep turning the skewers, turn the heat up 220 degrees last
5mins to Char the yogurt.
Check the chicken is fully cooked cut into the largest piece

Calories 308 per portion

CHICKEN GYROS

After our holiday to Greece a few years ago now I couldn't stop making or eating these I love them. Full of flavour and brings back so many memories whenever I eat them.

Another super easy recipe nothing too "faffy" if you are unsure when chicken is cooked cut into the biggest chunk, I still do this now just to be safe.

Pair this recipe with my Flatbreads which can be found in the SIDES section.

CHICKEN GYROS
INGREDIENTS SERVES 2

500g Chicken you can use thigh or breast
3 Tablespoons of 0% Fat Free Greek Yogurt
2 Teaspoons of Oregano
2 Teaspoons of Lazy Garlic
1 Teaspoon of Dried Mint
1 Teaspoon of Ground Cumin
Zest of Half a Lemon
Juice of Half a Lemon

Chop chicken into large chunks
Add the yogurt, oregano, dried mint, cumin, garlic and
lemon Zest and juice to a bowl and mix well
Taste the marinate is it to your liking? if not adjust
Add the chicken to the marinate and ensure its fully covered
Cover and place into the fridge for a minimum of 30minutes
longer if possible overnight would be best.
Thread the chicken onto skewers
Pop under the grill until cooked set the grill at 180 degrees
keep turning the skewers, turn the heat up 220 degrees last
5mins to Char the yogurt.
Check the chicken is fully cooked cut into the largest piece

Calories 309 per portion

PIZZA

When it comes to Pizza there is no way on a hot summers day I want to be faffing around making proper pizza dough, these flatbread pizza's work perfectly. They are quick to make with very few ingredients, what you decide to top them with is up to you, but whatever you choose they will be fab promise.

Please try and use thick Greek style yogurt especially if you have not made these before it really will make it easier for you to get the dough consistency right.

33

PIZZA

INGREDIENTS SERVES 2

80g Self Raising Flour
80g of 0% Fat Free Greek Yogurt
80g Mozzarella
2 Tablespoons of Tomato Puree
1 Teaspoon of Italian Herbs
Any toppings you like

Add the flour and yogurt to a mixing bowl
Use a spoon to mix them together they should start
to resemble "crumbs" once you get to this stage
use your hands to bring the dough together.
Roll into a ball and leave to sit for 10 mins
You can either make 1 big pizza or 2 smaller ones
from this dough.
Roll out your dough
Mix the tomato puree with 2 Teaspoons of water
mix well so it forms a smooth sauce.
Spread the tomato puree onto your pizza
Sprinkle with Italian herbs
Add the toppings of your choice
Top with Mozzarella
Pop into the oven on 180 degrees for 15mins or until
cooked this will depend on what toppings you have
used.

Calories 284 per portion ALL TOPPINGS EXTRA

BEEF BURGER

Who doesn't love a good beef burger?? I know we do and when the kids were little this is all I seemed to make especially when on holidays. For me burgers are fantastic especially for little ones as you can keep them plain to suit their tastes and maybe just add a sprinkle of salt and pepper

In this recipe I used a premade steak seasoning now I know this sounds ridiculous but burgers are really just lumps of steak and the seasoning I used worked really well. It does have a little heat kick to it probably from the black pepper so adjust the amount used if you are not keen on spicy foods.

BEEF BURGERS

INGREDIENTS SERVES 4

500g 5% Fat Minced Beef
1 Red Onion
2 Tablespoons of Schwartz Perfect Shake Steak

Pulse the onion in a blender into small pieces so it releases
some of it juices this is what will hold the burger
together
Add the onion and mince into a mixing bowl
Add the Steak spices
Mix everything together ensuring the spices are evenly
distributed throughout the mix
Divide the mixture into 4 and form burger shapes
Place into fridge for a minimum of 1 hour
Spray a large frying pan with oil on a medium heat
Add the burgers cook slowly
Once the bottom of the burger is "coloured" turn over
keep turning the burgers over until fully cooked
Ensure they are fully cooked and the centre of the
burger is hot.

Calories 160 per portion Swap in/out 18cals for seasoning

ZINGER BURGER

When you are looking for something a little different give this recipe a try, we loved it! It also makes a lovely change from Beef Burgers during the BBQ season.

This is a great one for the kids too that crunch of cornflakes works so well but you can swap it for breadcrumbs if you wish.

CHICKEN ZINGER BURGER

INGREDIENTS SERVES 2

400g Chicken Breast
50g Cornflakes
2 Teaspoons of Paprika
2 Teaspoons of Mild Chilli Powder
1 Teaspoon of Garlic Granules
1 Teaspoon of Onion Granules
1 Egg
Pinch of Salt & Pepper

Crush the cornflakes don't crush into fine dust leave some bigger pieces
Whisk the egg
Add all the spices and a pinch of salt and pepper
to the cornflakes and mix well
ensure they are mixed properly and distributed evenly
as you want the flavour in each bite.
Taste and adjust the mix if needed.
Dip the chicken into the egg then into the cornflakes
ensure its coated well
Spray top of chicken with spray oil
Place into oven on 180 degrees for 25-30 mins
turning half way to ensure base is cooked and the
cornflakes are crispy

Calories 278 per portion Swap in / out 83 cals for cornflakes

SUNDRIED TOMATO & GARLIC STUFFED CHICKEN

A bit of a Summer classic but one that I think can be easily overlooked especially if like me your head is full of burgers and kebabs as soon as the sun decides to shine.

I paired this with my Summer Salad recipe and the flavours together were fantastic especially with the optional dressing that goes with the salad.

SUNDRIED TOMATO & GARLIC STUFFED CHICKEN

INGREDIENTS SERVES 2

400g Chicken Breast
4 Tablespoons Philadelphia Lightest
20g Sundried Tomatoes
4 Bacon Mediallions
Half a Teaspoon of Lazy Garlic
3 Large Basil Leaves

Chop the sun dried tomatoes into small pieces
In a bowl mix the Philadelphia, garlic and sundried
tomatoes, taste and adjust if needed.
Cut a small slot into the chicken breast and gently
push the mixture into the slot but don't overload
as it will spill out during cooking.
Place 2 bacon medallions over each chicken breast
covering the slot you have made and secure it with
cocktail sticks to keep it in place
Cook in oven on 170 degrees keep the heat
slightly lower to ensure it cooks through evenly and
doesn't overheat the creamy mixture which can result
in it leaking from the chicken.
Cook for approx 25-30mins or until chicken is fully
cooked.

Calories 329 per portion

PORK & APPLE BURGER

I love these burgers when I first made them, I used apples but for me British apples just aren't sweet enough and all I could taste was grated apple, so I switched to using Apple Sauce such a brilliant swap as the sweetness with the pork works beautifully.

Pork mince can be coarsely ground so I have suggested you pulse it in a blender to break this down I have found that if you don't do this the burgers can fall apart easily whilst cooking.

PORK & APPLE BURGERS

INGREDIENTS SERVES 4

500g 5% Fat Minced Pork
3 Spring Onions
2.5 Tablespoons of Apple Sauce
A good pinch of Salt & Pepper

Pulse the spring onion, pork, apple sauce and salt
and pepper in a blender as this will help the burger hold
together as the pork mince can be very coarse which can
make the burger dry and fall apart.
DONT over blend it and turn it to "mush" it just
needs to break the pork mince up.
Divide the mixture into 4 and form burger shapes
Place into fridge for a minimum of 1 hour
Spray a large frying pan with oil on a medium heat
Add the burgers cook slowly
Once the bottom of the burger is "coloured" turn over
keep turning the burgers over until fully cooked
Ensure they are fully cooked and the centre of the
burger is hot.

Calories 167 per portion

KFC CHICKEN

I love making these "sharing platters" they are so easy and no fussing over plating up or who gets what, set it in the middle of the table and let everyone help themselves. They are also a great way of using up all those bits in the fridge that are looking a little sad for themselves.

As always with these spice blends they will come down to personal taste so test the spice mix and adjust if needed.

KFC CHICKEN

INGREDIENTS SERVES 2

500g Chicken Fillets
50g Cornflakes
1 Egg
1 Chicken OXO Cube
1 Teaspoon of Paprika
1 Teaspoon of Mild Chilli Powder
1 Teaspoon of Garlic Granules
1 Teaspoon of Onion Granules
Half a Teaspoon of Mustard Powder

Mix all the spices in a bowl and taste adjust if needed
Crush the cornflakes - not to dust make sure there
are smaller pieces and some larger pieces
Add the spices to the cornflakes and mix well ensure
they are distributed evenly
Whisk the egg
Dip the chicken into the egg then into the cornflakes
Place onto a baking tray sprayed with oil
Repeat until all chicken is used.
Spray top of chicken strips
Cook in oven on 170 degrees for 25-30mins
Turning over half way through cooking.

Calories 345 per portion Swap in/out 83cals for cornflakes

LIME & CORIANDER CHICKEN BURGERS

I appreciate this one sounds a bit of a funny combination but trust me it works. This recipe was created after a holiday in France and 2 weeks of eating beef burgers I'd had my fill of beef and wanted a lighter burger made from chicken and this was it!

The flavours work well together the key with this burger is deciding how much coriander to use, for me its not a problem I love the herb but if you're not too keen then only add as much as you can handle. What if you cannot handle coriander at all try swapping it for Thai Basil.

LIME & CORIANDER CHICKEN BURGER

INGREDIENTS SERVES 2

300g Chicken
Half An Onion
1 Teaspoon of Lazy Garlic
1 Bunch of Coriander
Half a Teaspoon of Salt
Half a Teaspoon of Pepper
Zest of Half a Lime

Dice the chicken if you are using breast
Add the chicken, salt and pepper, onion , zest of
lime, garlic and coriander to a blender and pulse
Dont over blend you only want to break the
chicken up if you blend it too much it will go to
mush and make it difficult for the burger to hold
together.
How much coriander you use is up to you if you have
no issues with it use approx 2 golf ball size amounts
Chicken can be really bland so season well
Form the chicken into 2 burger shapes
Place into the fridge to set for a minimum of 1 hour
Spray a pan with oil on a medium heat
Add the burgers cook slowly
Once the bottom of the burger starts to colour turn
it over and keep repeating until its fully cooked
Ensure the centre of the burger is fully cooked

Calories 174 per portion

BEEF KOFTAS

Yes these were as good as they look, absolutely delicious and I have finally perfected the technique to stop them falling off the skewers during cooking lol.

For me these types of fakeaway foods are what Lighter Bites and Summer food is all about easy prep easy cook food so you can kick back and enjoy.

KOFTAS

INGREDIENTS SERVES 4

500g 5% Fat Minced Beef
1 Onion
2 Teaspoons of Lazy Garlic
2 Teaspoons of Cumin
2 Teaspoons of Coriander
2 Teaspoons of Dry Mint
Half a Teaspoon of Paprika
Half a Teaspoon of Mild Chilli Powder
A pinch of Salt & Pepper

Blend the onion into small pieces so it releases its
juices as this is what will hold the koftas together
Mix the spices and taste adjust if needed
Add the onion and spices to the mince and mix
well ensure the spices are distributed evenly
throughout the mince
Take a golf ball size of the mix and "squish" it together
a couple of times this will smooth out the mixture
and help hold the koftas together during cooking
Roll the mix into a ball then roll into a "sausage shape"
Insert a BBQ skewer through the centre if using bamboo
make sure you soak it in water first
Place the koftas into the fridge for 1 hour
To cook place under a grill on 170-180 degrees
for 20-25mins

Calories 180 per portion (2 koftas) recipe makes 8 koftas

SLOW COOKER SECTION

I know lots of people come to the Summer months and put away their slow cookers – I'm not one of these people lol mine gets used all year round.

When we have hot days in the UK I don't want be stuck in the kitchen watching pans cook so wherever I can I use my slow cooker.

In this section I have created some easy Summer recipes that work well in the slow cooker if you don't have a slow cooker these recipes can also be cooked on the hob or in the oven.

SHARING PLATTERS – my favourite things to make they just save so much time and everyone gets to eat what they want, so no arguments. I have incorporated three platters into Lighter Bites using Beef, Chicken & Lamb and the recipes are really just ideas of how you can serve them, there is no hard and fast rules. Sharing platters are a fantastic way of using up all those bits in the fridge.

You can use leftover meat from Sunday Dinner if you have it to create any of the sharing platters.

TACOS – these were just wonderful, I know they can be cooked on the hob but to be honest they worked well in the slow cooker and when it came to dinner time it was simply a case of plating up.

I used a sachet mix which I bought from Tesco it was their own brand and very tasty it was too, I can see Tacos featuring heavily in my Summer cooking.

PAELLA- I'm not always a fan of paella as it seems to always be seafood and as you know I'm not a fan. So I decided to create my own using Prawns which I love and Chorizo which I also love.

Yes I used the slow cooker – we are back to my pet hate of standing watching pans cook I wasn't sure if it would work but it worked beautifully.

49

My top tip is as soon as the paella is cooked remove it from the slow cooker as the residual heat will keep cooking the rice and the rice will keep absorbing the liquid. You will end up with what I call "a claggy" mess on your hands – this a Northern technical term lol.

PULLED BEEF this is straight forward but I just wanted to add a note regarding gravy – us Brits do love our gravy! If you want a really thick rich gravy for the pulled beef I would suggest you add a sprinkle of gravy granules to thicken up the gravy, mine was fine but I know we are all different with regards to our love of gravy.

LEMON CHICKEN – this was beautiful perfect in every way easy prep easy cook. However, you may need to thicken the sauce and throughout Lighter Bites you will see I have suggested either Xanthan Gum or Cornflour mixed with cold water.

Xanthan gum can be found in the Free From isles in most supermarkets, if you are going to use this be careful you really do only need the smallest of amounts to thicken the sauce.

Where I have used xanthan gum, I used the tip of a teaspoon to thicken sauces – if you prefer to use cornflour feel free to do so.

TERIYAKI CHICKEN – a fantastic new slow cooker fakeaway recipe and so easy to make all ingredients are store cupboard too. In the recipe it talks about using chicken thighs and reducing the sauce this is something I have found out to my detriment this year.

For many years I always used chicken breast in any slow cooker recipes but over the last couple of years I have switched to chicken thighs, they are cheaper and don't dry out during cooking. However, if you are cooking a sauce that needs thickening you may find it difficult if you have used chicken thighs.

The fat that you either can't remove or see seeps into the cooking sauce and it can make it difficult to reduce the sauce. It can be done without adding any thickening agents you just need patience, a pan on a high heat and nerves of steel! If like me, you don't have patience then either use a very small amount of xanthan gum or cornflour sometimes these things are just not worth the stress.

What I will say is that the Teriyaki Chicken was amazing and worth trying when you are looking for something different to put on your weekly meal plan.

SPAG BOL – this is basically a bonus recipe for you as I have used it in my 10 minute lasagne recipe. For me spag bol just doesn't have to be served with spaghetti it can be so many different things which is why there is always 2 portions in my freezer for days when my fatigue is kicking my backside.

Some ideas for using spag bol would be, pasta bake, enchiladas, add to jacket potatoes, add them into a homemade taco bowl and top with cheese the options are endless.

SLOW COOKER PULLED BEEF

I have wanted to make this for years now and finally we are here this is such a fantastic easy recipe that can be adapted for different meal ideas.

Here I have served it as a sharing platter but it could easily be served as a Sunday Dinner type meal.

You can add gravy granules if you want a thicker gravy, I didn't need to do this but as always do whatever you feel is best for you.

SLOW COOKER PULLED BEEF
INGREDIENTS SERVES 4

800g Joint of Beef any cut
1 Onion any colour
1 Beef Stock Pot
2 Tablespoon of Worcester Sauce
250ml Water
Salt & Pepper

Finely slice onion and add to slow cooker
Add the joint of beef
Add Worcester sauce
Add Water
Cook on low 9-10 hours or until you can pull the beef apart with 2 forks
Once cooked pull the beef apart
Let it sit in the gravy and soak it up you may need to add a splash more water
Taste and season with salt & pepper

Calories 442 per portion

SLOW COOKER TACOS

This one is probably going to divide everyone who buys the book as you are either going to love it or hate the fact its cooked int the slow cooker –I loved it!

Yes you can easily do these in a pan on the hob but lets face it when the weather is good outside who wants to be indoors cooking – not me.

I cheated (what a shock) and used a packet taco mix from Tesco and to be honest it was really good, but you can make up your own spice mix if you wish.

SLOW COOKER BEEF TACOS
INGREDIENTS SERVES 4

500g 5% Fat Minced Beef
1 Sachet of Taco Seasoning the one i used was 30g in weight
Half a Red Onion
2 Teaspoons of Tomato Puree
100ml Water
Juice of Half a Lime

Finely slice onion and add to slow cooker
In a large frying pan sprayed with oil quickly brown
the mince then add to slow cooker
Add the Taco Seasoning
Add Tomato Puree
Add Water and mix well
Cook on low for 3-4 hours
Once cooked taste and add lime juice to suit your
taste as this will depend of the brand of Taco
Seasoning you have used.

Calories 167 per portion Swap in/out 24 cals for seasoning

SLOW COOKER CHICKEN TO ROAST CHICKEN

I think this is one of my favourite food hacks as it keeps the chicken super moist and during the warmer months you don't need to switch the oven on for hours to cook a chicken.

I wanted this in Lighter Bites as it works in so many different ways I have shown here how I would use it in a sharing platter but it work equally as a Sunday Dinner type meal too.

SLOW COOKER CHICKEN TO ROAST CHICKEN
INGREDIENTS

1 Chicken to suit the number of people you
are cooking for i usually use a 1.2-1.4kg chicken
for 2 with lots leftover to use in other dishes.
Any Vegetables you like or tin foil or ramekin

The chicken must be lifted off the bottom of the
slow cooker
I usually use a couple of carrots chopped up but
you can use tin foil scrunched up or a ramekin
turned upside down
Sit the chicken on the carrots or foil
Do not add any liquid
Add whatever spices or herbs you like
Cook on low for approx 6-7 hours for a 1.2-1.4kg
chicken
Use a digital meat thermometer to ensure the chicken
is fully cooked
Once cooked you can either leave it to cool and serve
as you wish OR...
Put it under a red hot grill to crisp and brown the skin
now you have roast chicken without all the "faff"

Calories will depend on size of chicken you use

LAMB SHARING PLATTER

Another of my favourite Summer meals you can use leftover lamb for this if you wish and you can use any cut of lamb it all cooks in the same way.

Ras El Hanout is a Middle Eastern spice which you can buy in most supermarkets it works well with beef too, if you have not used it before, start off with a small amount, taste and add more if you wish.

If you make this, I promise you will not be disappointed, I served mine with homemade flatbreads which you can find in the SIDES section of the book.

SLOW COOKER LAMB SHARING PLATTER
INGREDIENTS SERVES 4

1kg Lamb Any Joint
Carrots or Tin Foil or Ramekin
Water
Half a Tablespoon of Ras El Hanout Spice

Whatever you like to create your sharing platter
i used salad, red onion, tomatoes pomegranate seeds
garnished with coriander
Served with flatbreads and a mint yogurt dip
made from Fat Free Greet Yogurt and mint sauce
mixed.

The lamb must be lifted off the bottom of the
slow cooker i used a carrot chopped up you can
you tin foil scrunched up into balls or a ramekin
turned upside down.
Sit the lamb on top of the carrots
Add approx 100ml of water to the slow cooker
you really just need to cover the base.
Cook on low for 8-9 hours you want the meat
to fall apart
Once cooked allow it to cool slightly, then pull
it into strips
In a large frying pan sprayed with oil add the lamb
Add the Ras El Hanout spice mix the lamb and spices
together
TASTE you may want to add more spice.
Arrange your platter in whichever way you want.

Calories 438 per portion

SLOW COOKER GARLIC & LEMON CHICKEN

When you have been dreaming of a recipe like this for months and suddenly it appears on your plate and it did not disappoint. This shouted summer nights sat in the garden with a cheeky glass of fizz the perfect no fuss meal.

I have added a note into the recipe regarding thickening the sauce I used Xanthan gum if you decide to use this you only need the smallest of amount literally the tip of a teaspoon. Or you can use cornflour as always, the choice is yours.

SLOW COOKER GARLIC & LEMON CHICKEN
INGREDIENTS SERVES 4

650g Chicken Breast (4 Chicken Breasts)
1 Onion
1 Tablespoon of Honey
1 Lemon Zest & Juice of whole lemon
1 Teaspoon of Italian Herbs
1 Teaspoon of Lazy Garlic
Half a Vegetable Stock Pot
100ml Water

Dice the onion
Add the chicken to the slow cooker
Add the stock pot and water
Add Zest of a whole lemon together with the juce
Add Lazy garlic
Add Honey
Add Italian Herbs
Cook on low for 5-6 hours or until the chicken is fully cooked.
If you need to thicken the sauce you can either add Xanthan Gum find this in the Free From Isles in supermarkets or mix cornflour with cold water and add it to the slow cooker

Calories 216 per portion Thickening agents add as extra

SLOW COOKER PAELLA

Not a traditional Paella by any stretch of the imagination however it's a really good substitute. I wanted to add a white wine stock to this recipe but Tesco didn't have them in store on the day so I decided to just leave it out. You could add a small glass of wine if you wish.

For me it was perfect and so easy to make, and although not traditional worth trying.

SLOW COOKER PRAWN & CHORIZO PAELLA
INGREDIENTS SERVES 2

100g Arborio Rice or Orzo
1 Tin of Chopped Tomatoes OR 400g of Passata
Half an Onion
170g Cooked Prawns
50g Chorizo
50g Peas (I used frozen)
2 Teaspoons of Lazy Garlic
1 Teaspoon of Paprika
Half a Vegetable Stock Pot
200ml Water
Salt & Pepper to Taste

Finely dice the onion and in a large frying pan sprayed
with oil soften. If you dont have time for this step
miss it out but you may end up with crunchy
onions.
Add the onions to the slow cooker
Chop the chorizo into small pieces in a frying pan
sprayed with oil cook for 3-5 mins on high heat to
release the oils.
Add the chorizo to the slow cooker, deglaze the pan
with a dash of hot water to add all the oils from the
chorizo into the slow cooker
Add to the slow cooker the rice, the vegetable stock
pot and water
Add the garlic and paprika
Cook on low for 3-4 hours you may need to add more
water depending on which rice you use.
Add the cooked prawns and peas last 10minutes of cooking
Remove the paella from the slow cooker immediately as
the residual heat will keep cooking the rice and it will
keep absorbing all of the water.

Calories 437 per portion

SLOW COOKER LOADED POTATOES

How could I not put this recipe into Lighter Bites this is for me proper weekend food without the fuss. I always get asked what I would serve this recipe with for me it really goes with anything and would work well with the recipes within the FAKEAWAY section of the book.

SLOW COOKER LOADED POTATOES
INGREDIENTS SERVES 4

3 Large Baking Potatoes
1 Red Onion
3 Rashers of Bacon
300g Cheese i used Red Leicester
Tin Foil

Chop the potatoes into quarters
Thinly slice the onion
Remove any fat from the bacon
Grate the cheese
Line the slow cooker with 1 piece of tin foil then
use a 2nd piece going in the opposite direction
this forms a tin foil insert which allows you remove
the finished potatoes easily. It also keeps the
potatoes tightly packed and cooks them quicker
Ensure you have enough tin foil hanging over the edge
of the slow cooker to form a lid to cover the potatoes
Spray the foil with oil
Add a layer of potatoes, onions, bacon and cheese
Repeat as many times as you like
End with a cheese and bacon layer
Fold over the foil to cover the top layer
Cook on high 4-5 hours depending on the size of
your potatoes.
Once cooked lift out the tin foil insert and place
into an oven proof dish top with cheese and more bacon
if you wish place under a hot grill until cheese
is melted.

Calories 498 per portion

SLOW COOKER TERIYAKI CHICKEN

I made this recipe years ago in the slow cooker and whilst it was good it wasn't 100% but as with everything in life we learn as we move on and I can definitely say I have perfected this one.

The ease of this recipe is ridiculous and when you really fancy something different give this one a try.

SLOW COOKER TERIYAKI CHICKEN
INGREDIENTS SERVES 4

500g Chicken Breast or Thigh (I used Thigh)
4 Tablespoon of Dark Soy Sauce
4 Tablespoons of Honey
2 Tablespoons of White Wine Vinegar
1 Teaspoon of Ground Ginger

If you are using chicken thighs remove all visible fat
If you are using chicken breast leave it whole
Mix all the ingredients in a bowl and taste, adjust if needed
Add everything into the slow cooker
Cook on low 3-4 hours
Once cooked if using chicken breast pull the chicken
apart into slices
Thicken the sauce - add the sauce to a large frying pan
on a high heat, bring the sauce to a rolling bubble
and start to reduce it.
Once the sauce starts to thicken remove the pan from
the heat and let the honey solidify
Keep repeating this process until you get the consistency
of sauce you like.
If you are using thighs you may find it difficult to reduce
the sauce due any fat from the thighs being present in the
sauce. You can either add a very small amount of xanthan
gum or make up a cornflour mix with cold water.
I added the tip of a teaspoon of xanthan gum you really do
not need much so add sparingly
Add the chicken to the sauce and ensure the sauce coats
it fully.

Calories 212 per portion

SLOW COOKER SPAGHETTI BOLOGNESE

You will notice there is no picture for this recipe, im pretty sure we all know what spag bol looks like. The reason this recipe is in Lighter Bites is twofold.

One – it is a perfect easy summer meal, I mean who doesn't love spag bol??

Two – this is the base for the 10 minute lasagne recipe which you can find in the PASTA section of Lighter Bites.

SLOW COOKER SPAGHETTI BOLOGNESE
INGREDIENTS SERVES 4

500g 5% Fat Free Minced Beef
1 Tin Chopped Tomatoes or Passata
1 Onion
1 Tablespoon of Tomato Puree
2 Teaspoons of Lazy Garlic
1 Teaspoon of Italin Herbs
1 Oxo Cube
1 Red Wine Stock Pot OPTIONAL
A dash of Wocestershire Sauce
Any vegetables you like i usualy add mushrooms
and peppers
Basil as much as you like

Chop up all the vegetables you are using
In a large frying pan sprayed with oil soften the onion if you
don't have time for this you can miss this step but you may
end up with crunchy onions
Brown the mince again you can miss this step but i find
it helps the mince hold together better
Add everything into the slow cooker
DO NOT ADD ANY FURTHER LIQUID
Cook on low for 6-7 hours

Calories 201 per portion Add vegetables & Red wine Stock
Pot

SIDES SECTION

I wanted Lighter Bites to be a pick and mix type recipe book so you aren't left wondering what to add as a side dish to some recipes.

All the recipes within the sides section will work well with the Fakeaways, some of the Fish and Slow Cooker Section.

ROASTED VEGETABLES – I love roasted vegetables in the Summer and it's a great way of using up everything towards the end of the week before shopping day.

Although there is a recipe in Lighter Bites its one you can either follow or just ignore and throw in whatever you have that needs using up.

My top tip is don't overload the dish because you will steam the vegetables and not roast them – I have done this in my early days of cooking and let's face it no one likes "soggy veggies"

GARLIC BREAD – this is basically just my flatbread recipe made into a garlic bread. I know you can easily buy garlic bread from supermarkets but sometimes they can be stodgy this recipe is light and crispy.

You can make these as big or as small as you wish just adjust the amount of flour you use and use the same amount of Greek yogurt.

My top tip is to use thick Greek yogurt as its so much easier to work with and if this is the first time you are going to make these please don't use natural fat free yogurt. I used it on my first attempt at flatbreads and it ended up everywhere I was cover in sticky dough, sadly it ended up in the bin!

FLATBREAD – the same rules apply here as with the garlic bread use Greek yogurt. You can add any flavours you like to these flatbreads if I'm making kebabs, I usually make garlic and coriander flatbreads.

LOADED FRIES – the cheese sauce for these does sound weird but it works so well, they key is to not take your eyes off the pan. The cheese slices go from solid to liquid quickly, also once its cooked pour it straight over the fries as it solidifies as it cools which is great once its over the fries not so much when its still in the pan.

FLATBREADS

How could I not include these into Lighter Bites as they go so well with my all time favourite food Kebabs. However, they are so versatile as a base for other recipes such as Pizza or Garlic Bread.

FLATBREAD
INGREDIENTS SERVES 2

80g Self Rasing Flour
80g Greek Fat Free Yogurt
Any flavours you like (coriander, garlic etc)

Add the flour and any herbs, spices you are using
to a mixing bowl
Add the greek yogurt
Mix together to form a dough ball
Ensure you incoporate all the yogurt and flour before
you add any more yogurt
The dough should not be "sticky"
Leave to rest for 10 mins
Flour your surface
Split the dough into 2
Roll out into any shape you like
Don't roll the dough too thinly
Heat a large frying pan with no oil this pan should
be smoking hot
Add the flatbread to the pan
As soon as you see bubbles rise on the top of the
flatbread flip it over and repeat until the base
is cooked

Calories 154 per portion

SPICY SPUDS

Although I have called these Spicy Spuds they really aren't overly spicy they just have a little "kick", these will work with so many other recipes within the book.

As always you can adjust the seasoning to suit your tastebuds and if you are unsure then always start with less cook to say 70% and taste you can add more spice at this point, spray with more oil if you do this as it stops the spices tasting of powder.

SPICY SPUDS
INGREDIENTS SERVES 2

400g Potates any you like i used 2 baking potatoes
1 Teaspoon of Paprika
1 Teaspoon of Mild Chilli Powder
1 Teaspoon of Garlic Granules / Powder
1 Teaspoon of Onion Granules / Powder
Pinch of Salt

Chop the potatoes into small cubes
Use the microwave method to par boil them add the
potatoes to a microwave bowl add a small amount
of water then place a plate over the top. Microwave
on full power for 8 mins the potatoes should now
have some "give" to them.
Drain the potatoes and let them sit and steam for a
minute or two
Put them back in the microwave bowl and spray with
oil
Add the spices and give the potatoes and good shake
ensure they are all covered in the spice mix
Cook on 180 degrees for 20-30 mins or until cooked

Calories 237 per portion

LOADED FRIES

These were amazing we both loved these and it's a great way to jazz up chips or wedges perfect with a burger or pizza.

LOADED FRIES

INGREDIENTS SERVES 2

400g (2 Medium) Potatoes
2 Bacon Rashers
3 Light Cheese Slices
1 Spring Onion
Jalapeños OPTIONAL

Peel and chop the potatoes into chips / wedges
Par boil using the microwave method, add a small
amount of water to a microwave bowl add the
potatoes cover with a plate, place into microwave
on high for approx 10mins, drain and leave to steam for a
minute or two.
Spray with oil
Cook in the oven on 180 degrees for 25-30 mins
Grill the bacon until crisp then Chop into small pieces
Add the cheese to a saucepan and add 100ml water
keep the pan on a low heat and keep stirring the
cheese will melt and will start to resemble a sauce
once you get to this point take the pan off the heat.
If the cheese sauce becomes too thick add more water
add small amounts at a time.
Assemble your fries at the bottom of a serving dish
Sprinkle with bacon
Add the cheese
Chop the spring onion and sprinkle over the fries

Calories. 239 per portion

<u>SALSA</u>

Another brilliant side dish that works so well with so many recipes.

For me there is no exact recipe for Salsa it really can be a case of using up what you have in the fridge and making it to suit your tastebuds.

SALSA
INGREDIENTS SERVES 4

250g Cherry Tomatoes
1 Chilli
1 Small Red Onion
Zest of Half a Lime & Juice to suit your taste
Coriander to suit your taste
Salt

Finely dice tomatoes and onion
If you are not keen on heat / spice then leave the chilli
out. If you are using it finely dice it
Roughly Chop the Coriander add as much or as little
as you like
Add everything into a bowl and mix well
Add Zest of Half a lime
Add lime juice to suit your taste
Add salt - again add to suit your taste

Calories 26 per portion

GARLIC BREAD

This is basically my flatbread recipe made into a garlic bread and it tastes amazing. Such a quick and easy way to create a garlic bread plus you can add any other flavours you like – I nearly added cheese but had to stop myself, you know me and my love of cheese lol.

GARLIC BREAD

INGREDIENTS SERVES 2

50g Self Raising Flour
50g 0% Fat Free Greek Yogurt
2 Tablespoons of Flora Light
2 Teaspoons of Lazy Garlic
Rosemary to Garnish OPTIONAL

Add the flour and yogurt to a mixing bowl
Use a spoon to mix them together until they resemble
"crumbs" when you get to this point use your hands
to bring the dough together.
Roll into a ball and leave to sit for 10mins
Roll out the dough but don't roll it too thinly
In a microwave bowl add the Flora and heat in a
microwave until the margarine becomes liquid
Add the garlic mix well
Finely Chop rosemary if using it
Spread the garlic butter mixture over the garlic bread
Sprinkle the rosemary
Pop into ove 180 degrees for approx 10 mins

Calories 142 per portion

SUMMER ROASTED VEGETABLES

Although I have given you a written recipe for Roasted Vegetables it really is one of those recipes you can add anything too.

This is a perfect recipe for using up all those vegetables in the fridge that are destined for the bin.

ROASTED SUMMER VEGETABLES
INGREDIENTS SERVES 2

1 Aubergine
2 Courgettes
1 Red Onion
1 Pepper Any Colour
4 Garlic Cloves
3 Small Sprigs of Rosemary

Chop all vegetables
Add them to an ovenproof dish
Add the garlic but leave the skin on
Add the rosemary
Spray with oil
Top Tip - don't overload the dish or the vegetables
will steam rather than roast.
Cook in the oven on 180 degrees for 35-40minutes
Toss the vegetables half way during the cooking
and spray with more oil if needed
Once cooked sqeeze the garlic out of their outer
shell and mix into the vegetables
You could aslo add a squeeze of lemon if you wish.

Calories 73 per portion

PUDDINGS

Probably everyone's favourite section, I'm not a huge pudding fan but I will admit I really enjoyed making the ones in Lighter Bites.

None of them are super complicated or faffy as you know that's not my style plus, I wanted to create puddings that were quick to make. Again who wants to be standing for hours making puddings during the Summer months.

BREAD & BUTTER PUDDING – I'm not a fan of bread and butter pudding but I know lots are as I'm always asked for a recipe so here we are.

I did taste the recipe but for me this is the same problem with baked oats it's a texture thing. Graeme taste tested it for me and gave it a firm 10 out 10 so I'm taking his as a huge success.

CHEESECAKE PUD – born from the fact I couldn't be bothered to make the real thing lol. However, don't let the fact it looks too simple put you off as it tasted amazing and of course super easy to make.

TRIFLE this one is just in the book as a reminder of a low calorie easy pudding that really does hit the spot. I totally forget all about trifle, but I won't moving forward as I loved it plus you can make these ahead of time.

ORANGE CAKE – What beautiful Summer pudding we both loved this so much. My top tips with this recipe are the oranges again in the UK our oranges can lack flavour and if you use these types of oranges the flavour won't come through in the final cake.

For this reason, I added Marmalade which really did help boost the flavour in the cake. If you are confident the oranges, you are using are full of flavour then you can leave the marmalade out.

This isn't a traditional cake texture, but it is a really good substitute when you need something sweet. Two important tips, when you are whisking the eggs whites ensure they are mixed into stiff peaks you should be able to turn the mixing bowl over and they shouldn't move. Secondly when combining the whites to the batter mix ensure you cannot see any whites of the eggs trailing through the batter if you see this keep mixing.

LEMON CURD OATS – for me baked oats need to be baked for slightly longer than usual as I need the centre to be firm and not "squidgy" it's a texture thing which really put me off baked oats when first trying them. Adjust the cooking time to suit your taste.

FROYO CUBES – I love these I loved making them when the kids were little and making them again brought back so many memories. For this recipe I decided to make then in ice cube trays I just found it easier, but you can freeze the yogurt mix flat on baking tray if you wish.

FROYO CUBES

I used to make these when the kids were little but on a baking sheet, sadly they are all grown up, so I decided to make them in a smaller batch and in ice cube trays trust me its so much easier doing it this way.

These are the perfect when you want something sweet but don't want to blow you diet.

FROYO CUBES
INGREDIENTS MAKES 6

5 Tablespoons of 0% Fat Free Greek Yogurt
1 Tablespoon of Honey
100g Frozen Fruit
Half Teaspoon Vanilla Extract

Defrost frozen fruit and try to remove as much water
as possible
In a bowl mix the yogurt, honey and vanilla
Taste and make sure it's sweet enough for your taste
if not sweet enough add more honey
Add fruit to yogurt mix well
Spoon mixture into ice cube trays
Place into freezer until frozen

Calories 26 per portion (cube)

ORANGE CAKE

We loved this cake, it certainly didn't last long perfect with a cuppa sat in the sun. I have made this cake in the past but for me the issue is with the oranges in the UK they just don't ooze sweetness, so I have used orange extract and added marmalade to lift the orange flavour within the cake.

ORANGE CAKE
INGREDIENTS MAKES 14 SLICES

50g Self Raising Flour
5 Eggs
2 Tablespoons of Sweetener
Zest of Whole Orange
Juice of Half an Orange
4 Teaspoons of Orange Extract
1 Tablespoon of Orange Marmalade

Sieve Flour into bowl
Seperate eggs, yokes into flour whites into a seperate bowl.
To the flour add sweetener, orange extract, rind of orange and juice of orange.
Mix well so all ingredients are incorporated, taste the mixture is it sweet enough for your taste? If not add more sweetener
Whisk the egg whites into stiff peaks you should be able to turn the bowl over and the mix not fall out this is really important so take your time to get the whites mixed correctly.
Add 1/3rd of the egg whites to the batter and gently fold them in.
Add the remaining egg whites gently fold them in trying not to knock the air out of the mixture there should be no egg white trailing through the mix if there is keep folding.
Place mixture into a cake mould
Into oven 170 degrees for 25-30 mins depending on how hot your oven works

Calories 59 per portion (slice)

TRIFLE

I should be ashamed putting this recipe in Lighter Bites but no I am standing my ground on this one. As a child I loved trifle (minus the fresh cream, not a lover at all) but we forget these easy puddings that really do work their magic this is the first trifle I have had in years and I loved it! Plus, if you are watching your waistline these are the perfect pud.

RASPBERRY TRIFLE
INGREDIENTS MAKES 4

1 Jelly Sachet Raspberry
4 Mini Custard Pots
Raspberries as many as you like
60g Light Squirty Cream
Decorate as you wish

Make up the Jelly Sachet as per the manufacturers
instructions divide into 4 serving dishes
Add the raspberries to each dish if you want them to
float at the top let the jelly set slightly this will
stop them sinking to the bottom
Place into the fridge and leave to set
Once set add a mini custard pot to the top of each jelly
Top with 15g of Squirty cream
Decorate as you wish

Calories 85 per portion (each) using sugar free jelly.

CHEESECAKE PUD

Absolutely not a cheesecake but it makes a fantastic alternative without all the faff of waiting for it to set. Making an individual portion is also a great way of portion control perfect for dieting.

I loved this pudding and for someone who isn't a massive pudding fan I really enjoyed it.

CHEESECAKE PUD
INGREDIENTS SERVES 1

1 Digestive Biscuit
3 Tablespoons of Philadelphia Lightest
4 Tablespoons of 0% Fat Greek Yogurt
Half Tablespoon of Flora Light
1 Teaspoon of Vanilla Extract
Zest of Half a Lemon
Sweetener OPTIONAL to suit your taste

Use an individual ramekin type dish
Crush digestive
Melt butter and add it to the Digestive press this into
the bottom of the ramekin
Mix the Philadelphia and Greek Yogurt
Add vanilla extract
Add Zest of lemon and mix well
Taste - you may want to add sweetener to suit your
own personal taste
Place into refrigerator to chill for 1hour
Add any toppings you like

Calories 174 per portion

LEMON CURD BAKED OATS

If you follow me on any of my Social Media Channels you will know I'm not a huge baked oats fan it's the texture I don't like the "squidgyness" of them, sorry only word I can use to describe it.

However, I have found if you bake them for longer then the texture is much better, well it is for me anyway. My top tip is to decide how you like your oats and if you like a softer texture just reduce the cooking time.

LEMON CURD BAKED OATS
INGREDIENTS MAKES 1

40g Porridge Oats
3 Tablespoon of Fat Free 0% Greek Yogurt
1 Tablespoon of Lemon Curd
2 Tablespoons of Sweetener
1 Egg
Half a Teaspoon of Baking Power

Add the porridge oats, egg, yogurt, baking powder
sweetener into a mixing bowl mix well
Add 2/3rd of the mix into an ovenproof dish
Add 1 Tablespoon of Lemon Curd into the centre
Add the remaining mix ensure you cover the lemon
curd
Bake on 180 degrees for 15-25 mins depending on
how you like the texture of your baked Oats
I like mine firm in the middle so I bake them for
longer

Calories 294 per portion

BREAD & BUTTER PUDDING

If I told you that is the most asked for pudding recipe would you believe me??? Well, it's true. I'm not a fan of Bread & Butter Pudding it's the texture but I decided to give it a try as Graeme loves it.

All I will say is it past his taste test with flying colours so another successful recipe for all those who like bread & butter pudding but don't like the calories that go with it.

BREAD & BUTTER PUDDING
INGREDIENTS SERVES 1

60g Wholemeal Bread
2 Eggs
2 Tablespoons of 0% Fat Greek Yogurt
1 Tablespoon of Sweetener
2 Teaspoon of Vanilla Extract
1 Teaspoon of Lemon Zest OPTIONAL
15g Sultanas

Cut the bread into triangles and arrange in
an overproof dish.
Whisk the eggs, yogurt, vanilla extract, half a
tablespoon of sugar and lemon zest together
Pour the mixture over the bread and leave to
soak for 20 minutes
Add the sultanas
Sprinkle over half a tablespoon of sugar
Bake on 180 for 30-40mins the mixture should be
firm to touch.

Calories 363 per portion

I always like to put in a couple of pictures towards the end of the book to help see how the recipes can be presented in different ways.

Starting with spag bol here are some variations for you which will work well in the warmer months.

Traditional Spaghetti Bolognese

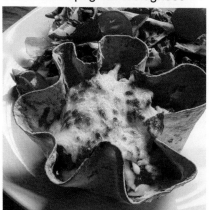

Tortilla wrap shaped into a bowl filled with spag bol and topped with cheese

Slow cooker chicken to roast chicken served as a Sunday Dinner type sharing platter

Slow cooker lamb served as a Sunday Dinner type sharing platter.

The last page is dedicated to my "wonderful other half" who has helped me achieve my dreams.

He has never once commented on the state of the kitchen during the cooking of all the food within Lighter Bites. Trust me it's not been a pretty sight, but at least I didn't set anything on fire this time – always a great win in my book!

I hope you have enjoyed the recipes within Book no2 and hopefully I will see you on my live cooking tutorials on Facebook.

Bon Appetite xx

Printed in Great Britain
by Amazon